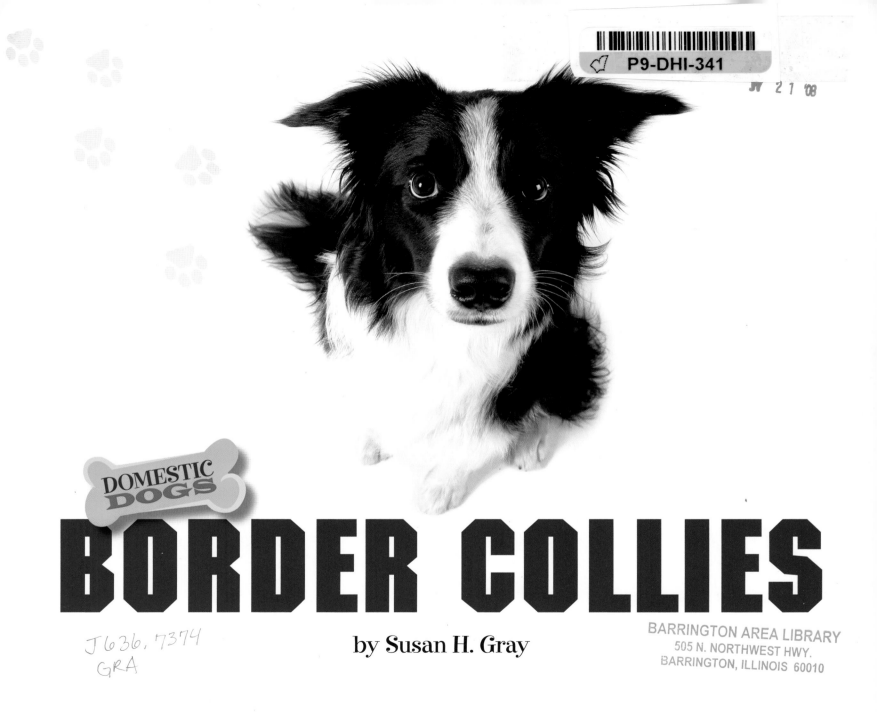

DOMESTIC DOGS

BORDER COLLIES

by Susan H. Gray

Published in the United States of America by The Child's World®
PO Box 326 • Chanhassen, MN 55317-0326
800-599-READ • www.childsworld.com

PHOTO CREDITS
© Andraz Cerar/BigStockPhoto.com: 19
© Arco Images/Alamy: 15
© Ashley Cooper/Alamy: 23
© imagebroker / Alamy: cover, 1
© Jason Smalley/Wildscape/Alamy: 9
© Mark Raycroft/Minden Pictures: 13, 21, 29
© PhotoStockFile/Alamy: 27
© tbkmedia.de/Alamy: 17
© Tom Kidd/Alamy: 25
© Tony West/Corbis: 11

ACKNOWLEDGMENTS
The Child's World®: Mary Berendes, Publishing Director;
Katherine Stevenson, Editor

Content Adviser: Susane Hoffman, Sheepy Corner Farm (www.sheepycorner.com)

The Design Lab: Kathleen Petelinsek, Design and Page Production

LIBRARY OF CONGRESS CATALOGING-IN-PUBLICATION DATA
Gray, Susan Heinrichs.
  Border collies / by Susan H. Gray.
      p. cm. — (Domestic dogs)
  Includes bibliographical references and index.
  ISBN 1-59296-772-8 (library bound : alk. paper)
  1. Border collie—Juvenile literature. I. Title. II. Series.
  SF429.B64G73 2007
  636.737'4—dc22   2006022635

Table of Contents

NAME That DOG!

What **breed** of dog loves to work? 🐾 What dog can take care of other animals? 🐾 What dog sometimes works at airports? 🐾 What dog might have one brown eye and one blue eye? 🐾 Did you guess the **border** collie? 🐾 Then you are correct!

5

Some Very Smart Dogs

Long ago, many people in Great Britain (BRIH-tun) kept sheep. Some people had hundreds of sheep. Caring for the sheep was hard work. People started using dogs to help. They taught the dogs to **protect** the sheep. They taught them to keep the flocks of sheep together.

People in different areas used different kinds of dogs. In Wales, they used sheepdogs. In Scotland, they used collies.

Great Britain is an island in Europe. It includes England, Scotland, and Wales. The map on the left shows where Great Britain is on Earth. The map on the right shows a closer view.

Atlantic Ocean

Scotland

North Sea

Northern Ireland

Ireland

England

Wales

Great Britain

Atlantic Ocean

English Channel

France

7

Some people lived on the border between England and Scotland. Their dogs became known as "border collies." These hard-working dogs could tend sheep all day.

In 1876, one man had wonderful border collies. He wanted to show them off. He asked people to come watch the dogs work. He put a hundred sheep in a field. He led three of the sheep far away. Then he told his dogs to get busy. The dogs brought the three sheep back to the flock. Then they moved the whole flock into a pen. Everyone was amazed!

Since then, more and more people have gotten border collies. Most people put the dogs to work herding sheep and other animals. Others keep them as pets.

Border collies are called herding dogs because they herd other animals. German shepherds and Old English sheepdogs are herding dogs, too.

This border collie is herding sheep in Yorkshire, England.

Good Looking and Sporty

Border collies are medium-sized dogs. They are not heavy, but they are strong. They are about 20 to 22 inches (51 to 56 centimeters) tall at the shoulder. Adults weigh about 30 to 40 pounds (14 to 18 kilograms).

These dogs are full of energy. They are very **athletic**. They love to go jogging with their owners. They are great at catching tennis balls. When they run, they can speed up very quickly. They can turn quickly, too. Border collies can run and exercise for hours!

Border collies love to run! This dog is exercising with its owner.

Some border collies have very smooth coats. These dogs stay cleaner than those with rougher coats. They stay cooler in hot weather, too.

Border collies have thick, double coats. When you pet a border collie, you can feel its top coat. The top coat has straight or wavy hair. If you dig in deeper, you can feel the undercoat. The undercoat has short, fluffy hair.

Border collies come in different colors. Some of them are black. Others are black and white. Others have dark or light brown hair. Some even have silver-gray coats. The silver-gray coats are called "blue."

Border collies' ears stick up. The ends tip over just a bit. The dogs' eyes are either brown or blue. Some border collies have one brown eye and one blue eye!

Both of these dogs are border collies. Which color do you like better?

Round Them Up!

Border collies love to work. Their favorite job is herding other animals. They use some tricks to keep the animals together. One trick is to walk very low to the ground. The dogs look as if they are **stalking** the animals. This keeps the animals from walking off alone. They are afraid the dogs might jump on them! The dogs would never do that, though. They know not to attack.

This border collie is herding geese on a farm.

Another trick is called "giving eye." The collie stares hard at an animal. The stare is enough to keep the animal in line.

Most people do not have sheep that their dogs can herd! Instead, border collies often try to herd other things. They might herd other pets. They might even round up family members.

Some border collies do other things to keep busy, too. They go running or hiking with their owners. They learn to run tracks and jump fences. Border collies are always ready to learn new things. Even old border collies like to learn new tricks.

Dogs that herd sheep learn many **commands**. Trainers teach them to "walk on" or "take time." "Walk on" means to walk toward the sheep. "Take time" means to slow down.

What do you think this border collie is staring at?

Border Collie Babies

Border collie mothers usually have about six puppies in a **litter**. The puppies have round little noses. They have short, soft hair. They have tiny claws. Their eyes are not open yet. Their tiny ears cannot hear. Their legs are too weak for walking.

At birth, each puppy weighs about 10 to 12 ounces (284 to 340 grams). That is about as heavy as an apple. Within two weeks, the puppies grow to twice that size.

This border collie puppy is only a few days old. She has the "blue" coloring.

Puppies should spend their first few weeks with their littermates. It makes them feel safe. It also helps them learn how to be with other dogs. People should not **adopt** puppies less than eight weeks old.

A lot happens in a puppy's first month. Its eyes open, and it begins to look around. It begins to hear things. Its baby teeth start to come in. Its legs grow stronger. The puppy starts to stand and run around.

The puppy also starts to play with its brothers and sisters. Sometimes the puppies bite each other. Those sharp little teeth hurt! But the puppies can also bark. A puppy's loud yelp is like shouting "Stop it!" This is how puppies learn to get along with each other.

These border collies are just a few weeks old.

Border Collies at Home and at Work

Border collies are so smart, they can do many jobs. In many places, they still look after sheep and cattle. They keep the animals together. They move the animals where they need to go. Two good dogs can do the work of several people.

Some border collies have different jobs instead. Some help people who are deaf or blind. They lead their owners across busy streets. They let them know when the doorbell or phone rings. They let them know when someone comes up the driveway.

This border collie is a search-and-rescue dog. It helps find people who have been trapped in earthquakes or by storms.

SEARCH & RESCUE

Some border collies even work at airports. Airports usually have lots of land. Sometimes birds come to the airports to feed. The birds can be a problem for airplanes. They can even make the planes crash! Some airports bring in border collies. The dogs spend all day chasing the birds away. They do not hurt the birds. They just keep them away from the planes.

A border collie in Ohio works at a golf course. She spends her day chasing geese away. She also likes to ride in the golf carts.

Border collies often work with the police. They can help find people who are missing.

This border collie is in training. It is learning to rescue people who have been trapped under snow.

25

Caring for a Border Collie

Most border collies live long, healthy lives. They can live to be 14 or 15 years old. Some get hip problems as they get older. Their leg bones pop out of their hip bones. Animal doctors, called **veterinarians**, can help treat this problem.

Some border collies are born with eye problems. Sometimes, these problems make the dogs go blind. But usually, they do not hurt the dogs' eyesight. Veterinarians can check puppies for eye problems.

This veterinarian is checking a border collie for hip problems.

Border collies need something to do! Their owners must find ways to keep them busy. This can be hard for people who work all day. It can be hard for people who have no yard.

A border collie that is bored will tear things up. It might chew on a sofa or tear up shoes. People who have border collies must pay attention to them. They must make sure the dogs get outside and run around. They need to teach the dogs some tricks. If they do, the dogs will be happy and lively. And happy border collies are a joy to be around!

In the summer, border collies can get too hot. Their heavy coat keeps them too warm. Owners should not leave their dogs in hot cars. They should not let them run around on hot days.

This border collie is taking a short rest after playing.

Glossary

adopt (uh-DOPT) To adopt a child or animal is to take it in as your own. Puppies are adopted after they are six weeks old.

athletic (ath-LEH-tik) Someone who is athletic is very good at sports. Border collies are athletic dogs.

border (BOR-dur) A border is an imaginary line between two countries or areas. Border collies came from the border between England and Scotland.

breed (BREED) A breed is a certain type of an animal. There are many breeds of dogs, including border collies.

commands (kuh-MANDZ) Commands are orders to do certain things. Border collies can learn lots of commands.

litter (LIH-tur) A litter is a group of babies born to one animal at the same time. Border collies' litters usually have about six puppies.

protect (pruh-TEKT) To protect something is to keep it safe. Border collies sometimes protect other animals.

stalking (STAH-king) Stalking is hunting quietly and secretly. Border collies sometimes look as if they are stalking other animals.

veterinarians (vet-rih-NAIR-ee-unz) Veterinarians are doctors who take care of animals. Veterinarians are often called "vets" for short.

To Find Out More

Books to Read

American Kennel Club. *The Complete Dog Book for Kids*. New York: Howell Book House, 1996.

Gebauer, Roland, Cheri Bladhold, and W. Phillip Keller. *Lass*. Grand Rapids, MI: Kregel Kidzone, 2004.

Hobbs, Valerie. *Sheep*. New York: Farrar, Straus, and Giroux, 2006.

Voight, Cynthia, and Tom Leigh (illustrator). *Angus and Sadie*. New York: HarperCollins, 2005.

Places to Contact

American Kennel Club (AKC) Headquarters
260 Madison Ave, New York, NY 10016
Telephone: 212-696-8200

On the Web

Visit our Web site for lots of links about border collies:

http://www.childsworld.com/links

Note to Parents, Teachers, and Librarians: We routinely check our Web links to make sure they're safe, active sites—so encourage your readers to check them out!

Index

About the Author

Susan H. Gray has a Master's degree in zoology. She has written more than 70 science and reference books for children. She loves to garden and play the piano. Susan lives in Cabot, Arkansas, with her husband Michael and many pets.

CRAB

LIVING THINGS

CRAB

Rebecca Stefoff

BENCHMARK BOOKS

MARSHALL CAVENDISH
NEW YORK

Benchmark Books
Marshall Cavendish Corporation
99 White Plains Road
Tarrytown, New York 10591-9001

Illustrations by Steven James Petruccio

Library of Congress Cataloging-in-Publication Data
Stefoff, Rebecca, date.
Crab / by Rebecca Stefoff.
p.   cm. — (Living things)
Includes index.
Summary: Examines the physical characteristics, life cycle,
and natural habitat of different types of crabs.
ISBN 0-7614-0444-9 (lib. bdg.)
1 Crabs—Juvenile literature. [1. Crabs.]
I.Title. II. Series: Stefoff, Rebecca, date.   Living things.
QL444.M33S665 1998   597.3'86—dc21   97-9130 CIP AC

Photo research by Ellen Barrett Dudley

Cover photo: *The National Audubon Society Collection/Photo Researchers, Inc.,*
Mike Neumann

The photographs in this book are used by permission and through the courtesy of:
Animals Animals: John L. Pontier, 2, 13; James D. Watt, 6-7; E.R. Degginger, 10;
Oxford Scientific Films/Colin Milkins, 23 (top); G.I. Bernard, 23 (bottom); Fritz
Prenzel, 27; C.C. Lockwood, 32. *The National Audubon Society Collection/Photo
Researchers, Inc.*: Tom McHugh, 8, 10-11, 15, 19 (right); F. Stuart Westmorland,
11 (bottom); George Holton, 14; Gregory Ochocki, 16; Andrew J. Martinez, 16-17;
Andrew G. Wood, 19 (left); E.R. Degginger, 20; Dr. Paul A. Zahl, 22; Mandal Ranjit,
24 (right); Adam Jones, 26-27. *Peter Arnold*: Marilyn Kazmers, 9; Kelvin Aitken,
11 (top right); Bob Evans, 12; Fred Bavendam, 17, 18; Matt Meadows, 21 (left);
J. Cancalosi, 21 (right); Roland Sietre, 24 (left); Norbert Wu, 25.

Printed in the United States of America

3   5   6   4   2

For Sue Fleming, who loves the beach

crab with sea anemone, Indonesia

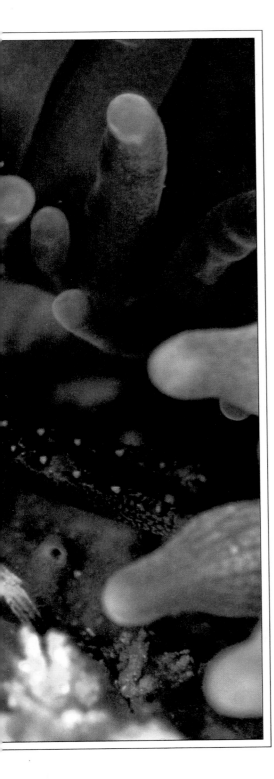

A crab peeks out of its hiding place and watches the world with its big red eyes.

This crab's world is the ocean floor. But you could find a crab on land, or even up a tree! Crabs are full of surprises.

shame-faced crab, Atlantic Ocean

A crab has a hard shell on the outside instead of bones on the inside. When a crab tucks in its legs, it's all shell. If you didn't see its shiny eyes, you might think it was a rock.

Crabs' eyes are on stalks. If the stalks are long enough, a crab can wave its eyes around and look in two directions at once.

red hermit crab in sponge, Caribbean Ocean

S ome crabs walk across the sea bottom on short fat legs. Others have long skinny legs. On all crabs, the front pair of legs is special. These legs end in claws, or pincers. Crabs use their pincers like hands to pick up things and hold them.

All crabs have ten legs. You can't always see all ten, though. Crabs sometimes tuck their back legs

arrow crab, Bahamas

up under their bellies.
Crabs that can swim have
back legs that look like little
paddles. When you're
counting legs, remember—
the pincers and paddles are
legs, too.

young king crab, Puget Sound

crabs fighting

Crabs fight with their pincers. They try
to flip each other over or break each other's
legs. If you ever try to pick up a crab, be
very careful. It might pinch you, and its
pincers are strong. The best way is to pick a
crab up by the shell, behind its back legs.

Fiddler crabs have one pincer that's much
bigger than the other. Two male crabs try to
scare each other by waving their big pincers
in the air. And when a male crab wants to
meet a female, he waves his pincer to get
her attention.

12

male fiddler crabs fighting, Florida

What else do crabs do with their pincers? They gather food. Some crabs eat plants. Others eat fish or snails or the small animals that live in seashells. Many crabs eat dead animals or plants. They are part of nature's "clean-up crew."

scarlet crab eating algae, Galapagos Islands

spotted pebble crab eating miter shell

sheepshead crab, California

There are nearly five thousand different kinds of crabs. Most of them are marine animals. This means that they live in the sea. There are crabs in all the oceans of the world, from the cold, dark waters around the North and South Poles to coral reefs in warm tropical seas.

toad crab, Gulf of St. Lawrence

Australian crabs

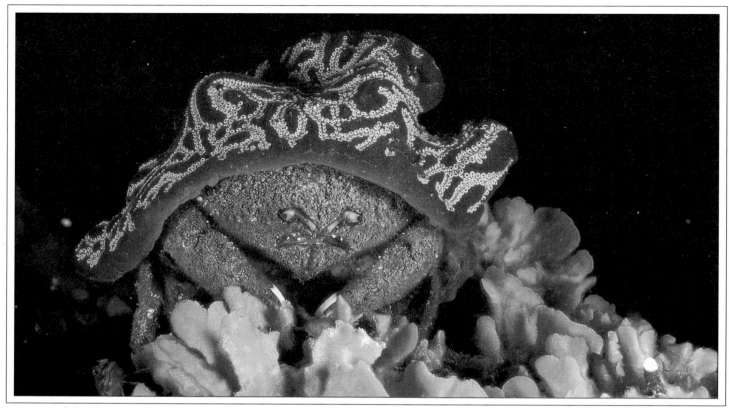

sponge crab wearing sea squirt, Australia

These crabs are called decorator crabs. They decorate themselves by putting sponges, seaweed, and other things on their backs. The "decorations" are really disguises. They help hide the crabs from turtles, fish, and seals that like to eat them.

Decorator crabs wear all kinds of disguises. Some cover themselves with living animals such as sea squirts. Others wear plants. Look at the little kelp crab on the green leaf. It lives on kelp, a huge undersea plant. Its disguise is a fuzzy coat the same color as the kelp. The fuzz is really many small plants called algae. They grow right on the crab's shell.

collector crab, Indonesia   *kelp crab, northern Pacific Ocean*

mountain crab

Not all crabs are marine creatures. Some live on land, usually in the warmer parts of the world. But land crabs must go into water to have babies. All young crabs spend the first part of their lives in water.

The biggest land crab is the coconut crab. It lives in the tropics, where coconuts grow on palm trees. Coconut crabs use their huge, strong pincers to climb trees, searching for soft plants and fruit to eat. They also eat dead animals.

coconut crab

red land crab, West Indies

Hermit crabs don't have hard shells of their own, so they live in the shells left behind by snails and sea creatures. Wherever a hermit crab goes, it drags its home around with it. When a hermit crab gets too big for its home, it finds a bigger shell and moves in.

hermit crab moving to bigger shell

land-dwelling hermit crab

Indian Ocean crab

beach crab, India

Some crabs live on beaches—or under them. They dig nests in the sand with their claws.

Crabs look for food at the edges of the waves. They also watch for signs of danger, such as seagulls overhead. Seagulls love to eat crabs. But at the first sign of trouble, the crabs run back to their holes. You'd be surprised to see how fast a crab can burrow into the sand.

ghost crab, Seychelles Islands

purple shore crab, Olympic Peninsula

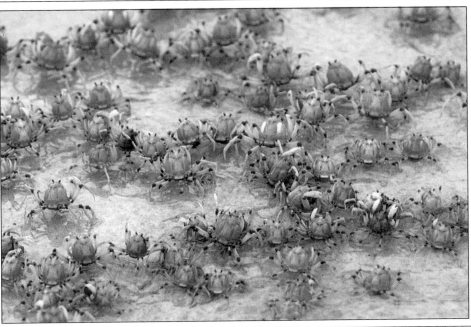

soldier crabs, Australia

Crabs scamper across beaches. They clamber over rocks and reefs pounded by the waves. They prowl tide pools with their pincers up, ready to grab their next meal. Someday, when you're walking on a beach, you may meet a crab where the water meets the land.

A QUICK LOOK AT THE CRAB

Crabs belong to a large group of mostly sea-dwelling animals called crustaceans (krus TAY shuns). Lobsters, shrimp, and crayfish are also crustaceans. Crabs are found in almost every part of the sea; some kinds live on land in the warmer regions. Scientists divide crabs into two big groups. One group, the true crabs, contains more than 4,500 species, or different varieties. The other group, the hermit crabs, contains several hundred species. Crabs molt, or shed their skins, as they grow. After a crab molts, it is covered with soft skin that soon hardens and becomes its new shell. Hermit crabs have long, soft abdomens which they protect by wearing snail shells or seashells.

Here are six kinds of crabs, along with their scientific names and a few key facts.

PACIFIC SAND CRAB

Emerita analoga
(ay meh REE tuh an uh LO guh)
Body measures about 1.4 inches (3.5 cm) across. Usually gray in color. Has been found from Chile to Alaska but is rare north of Oregon. Found only burrowed into sandy, wave-swept beaches. Is eaten by many birds and fish.

STRIPED SHORE CRAB

Pachygrapsus crassipes
(pak ee GRAP sus CRAH see pays)
Body measures 2 inches (5 cm) across. Lives on Oregon and California beaches. Climbs and scurries around on rocks, hunts in and out of water.

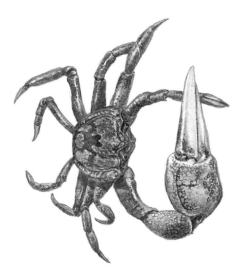

CALIFORNIA FIDDLER CRAB
Uca crenulata
(YEW cuh cren yew LAH tuh)
One of about 60 species of fiddler crabs found in warm regions of the world, where they live in burrows on beaches. Male fiddler crabs have one claw that is much larger than the other. They use it when fighting with other males and wave it to attract females.

GREEN CRAB
Carcinus maenas
(car CEE nus MEE nus)
Body is 3 to 3.5 inches (8–9 cm) across. Found off coasts of Europe, North America, South Africa, and Australia. Lives on sea bottom in up to 20 feet (6 m) of water. Eats clams and mussels.

DUNGENESS CRAB
Cancer magister
(CAN ker MAG iss ter)
Body is 7.5 to 9 inches (19–23 cm) across. Old reports describe much larger specimens not found today. Lives in beds of eelgrass in shallow water from California to Alaska. Eats clams, small crabs, and fish.

29

JAPANESE SPIDER CRAB
Macrocheira kaempferi
(mak roh KAY ee ruh KEEMP feh ree)
Largest known crab in the world. Can have leg span of 12 feet (3.6 m).
Lives on sea bottom in North Pacific Ocean.

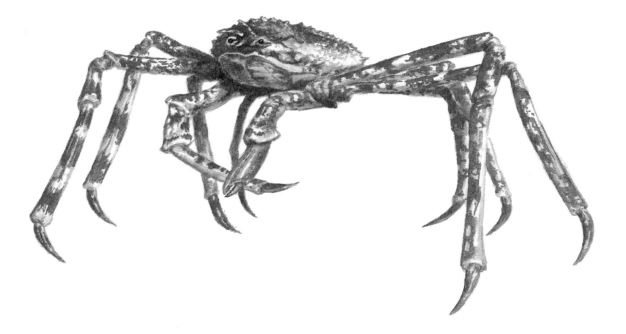

Taking Care of the Crab

Some crabs need our protection. When people build homes or other buildings, pollute water, and destroy coral reefs, they disturb the beaches, tide pools, or forests where crabs live. Sometimes people catch too many crabs, or take so many fish or mussels that the crabs may not find enough to eat. Crabs are a vital part of the network of life in our world's waters and on its beaches. It is up to us to protect them and the places where they live.

Find Out More

Bailey, Donna. *Crabs*. Austin, TX: Steck-Vaughn, 1991.

Bailey, Jill. *Discovering Crabs and Lobsters*. New York: Bookwright Press, 1987.

Cooper, Jason. *Crabs*. Vero Beach, FL: Rourke Publications, 1996.

Johnson, Sylvia A. *Crabs*. Minneapolis: Lerner Publications, 1982.

——————-. *Hermit Crabs*. Minneapolis: Lerner Publications, 1989.

Kite, Patricia. *The Crab*. Morton Grove, IL: Whitman, 1994.

Index

Rebecca Stefoff has published many books for young readers. Science and environmental issues are among her favorite subjects. She lives in Oregon and enjoys observing the natural world while hiking, camping, and scuba diving.

ghost crab, Massachusetts